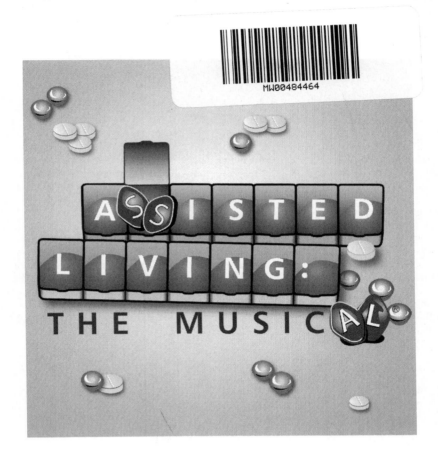

Book & Lyrics by
Rick Compton & Betsy Bennett

Music by
Rick Compton & Betsy Bennett
(unless otherwise noted)

STEELE SPRING
STAGE RIGHTS

www.stagerights.com

ASSISTED LIVING: THE MUSICAL

For all stage performance inquiries, please contact:

Steele Spring Stage Rights
3845 Cazador Street
Los Angeles, CA 90065
(323) 739-0413
www.stagerights.com

CAST OF CHARACTERS

Cast Total: 1F, 1M (flexible)

THE MAN: (Bari-tenor, B3b to F4) is a 55+ active retiree. Everyman, in Bermuda shorts.

THE WOMAN: (Alto, E3 to E5b) is a 55+ active retiree. A frisky optimist with a secret tattoo.

RANDY MAN: (Baritone, F3 to F4) is a 55+ ladies' man with a power problem.

NAOMI LIPSCHITZ-YAMAMOTO-MURPHY: (Mezzo, G3 to B5b) is a 55+ nicotine-drenched real estate yenta whose clients want to get their hands on more than just real estate... or so she believes. She shows 'em around The Roost and she's always on the lookout for an upgrade, as her last names would imply.

HUNGRY MAN: (Bari-tenor, C4 to F4) is a 55+ beta male with a biting issue.

COMPUTER WOMAN: (Mezzo, G3 to F4 (C5 optional)) is a 55+ spinster librarian who suffers online heartbreak.

THE LAWYER: is a 55+ half-Southern Baptist preacher, half-used car salesman, half-carney.

NURSE: (Mezzo, G3 to B5) is any age, devoted and direct to a fault.

DOCTOR (Bari-tenor, G3 to F4) is any age, comedic and sales-y.

BEN YOUNGER: is a 55+ over-the-top Borscht-Belt comedian.

COUNTRY CLUB WOMAN: (Soprano, C4 to D5) is a 55+ newly retired Junior Leaguer.

COUNTRY CLUB MAN: (Tenor, C3 to D4) is a 55+ newly retired Captain of Industry.

WALKER MAN: (Tenor, F3 to A4) is a 55+ active golfer.

WALKER WOMAN: (Mezzo, D4 to A5) is a 55+ active, spunky flasher... sorta.

SLEAZY MAN: (Baritone (Bass), C3 to D4) is a 55+ lounge lizard... and proud of it.

SETTING

At Pelican Roost, an active, over-55 full service retirement community, in the present.

RUN TIME

One act, no intermission, 75 minutes

SCENES

PRELUDE

House fades to black.

Stage fades to black.

PIANIST enters, plays ethereal arpeggios. Blue light floods the stage, as if in... heaven.

MAN and WOMAN enter.

WOMAN: Is this it?

MAN: I think it is.

WOMAN: The afterlife.

MAN: It must be. I don't have gas any more.

WOMAN: The last thing I remember, we were at Pelican Roost, our over-55 community.

MAN: And our wonderful son was standing over us.

WOMAN: He wasn't all that wonderful. You know your vintage corvette?

MAN: Yes?

WOMAN: That's why he pulled the plug, dear.

MAN: No!

WOMAN: Pelican Roost... the best years of our lives.

Light change and song begins.

SCENE 1

MAN & WOMAN:
EVERYTHING IS SWELL WHEN YOU'RE IN PELICAN ROOST.
NO MATTER HOW YOUR DOIN', WE'LL GIVE A BOOST.
SUNSHINE AND FREE-TIME

WOMAN:
HAPPY HOUR TOO.

MAN & WOMAN:
WE'RE DANCING THE WATUSI AND THE HULLABALOO
EVERYTHING IS SWELL WHEN YOU'RE IN PELICAN ROOST.
EVERYONE WHO LIVES THERE IS THE TOPS.

WOMAN:
WE GOT ARTIFICIAL FLOWERS

MAN:
AND GRAB-BARS IN THE SHOWERS.

MAN & WOMAN:
EVERYTHING IS PELICAN ROOST.

WOMAN:
THERE'S ALWAYS ROOM AT MAH JONG, WE'LL TEACH YA HOW TO PLAY.

MAN:
THE FISH I CATCH AT LUNCH, CAN BE TONIGHT'S FILLET

WOMAN:
IN A CREAMY BESCHAMAEL,
    (To audience)
HE'S LEARNED HOW TO COOK!

MAN:
I CAN WORK IT OFF TOMORROW

WOMAN:
RIGHT.

MAN:
OR JUST READ A BOOK

MAN & WOMAN:
EVERYTHING IS SWELL WHEN YOU'RE IN PELICAN ROOST.
NO MATTER HOW YOUR DOIN', WE'LL GIVE A BOOST.
SWIMMING AND GOLFING

WOMAN:
A MANI-PEDI, TOO

MAN & WOMAN:
WE'RE SOAKIN' IN THE HOT TUB, TAKIN' IN THE VIEW
EVERYTHING IS SWELL WHEN YOU'RE IN PELICAN ROOST.

MAN & WOMAN (CONT'D):
EVERYONE WHO LIVES THERE IS THE TOPS.

WOMAN:
SKINNY DIPPING IN THE POOL.

MAN:
IT AIN'T PRETTY BUT IT'S COOL.

MAN & WOMAN:
EVERYTHING IS PELICAN ROOST.

WOMAN:
I WON A CAR WASH AT THE WEEKLY PUB NITE QUIZ

MAN:
I PLAYED THE ROLE OF DOROTHY IN OUR PRODUCTION OF THE WIZ.

WOMAN:
OUR LIVES ARE FREE OF WORRY. FULL OF PARTY, FUN AND FRIENDS

MAN & WOMAN:
WE DON'T CARE WHAT IT MEANS CUZ IT JUSTIFIES THE END.
EVERYTHING IS SWELL WHEN YOU'RE IN PELICAN ROOST.
NO MATTER HOW YOUR DOIN', WE'LL GIVE A BOOST.
DINING AND DANCING

WOMAN:
AND HOOCHY COOCHY COO!

MAN & WOMAN:
WE SHUCKED OFF OUR PAST AND OUR INHIBITIONS TOO!

EVERYTHING IS SWELL WHEN YOU'RE IN PELICAN ROOST
EVERYONE WHO LIVES THERE IS THE TOPS.
WE'VE GOT HEARING AIDS AND GLASSES.
WE AIN'T SITTING ON OUR ASSES

MAN:
WE'RE LOVIN' WHEN WE GET THE YEN.

WOMAN:
CUZ I SUPPLEMENT MY ESTROGEN.

MAN & WOMAN:
EVERYTHING IS PELICAN ROOST.
WELCOME TO THE ROOST!

MAN exits.

SCENE 2

SONG #2: HELP! I'VE FALLEN (FOR YOU) AND I CAN'T GET UP

WOMAN: You know, aging is a lot better than I thought it was going to be. It's like being in my twenties but with no alarm clocks, no pregnancy and the drugs are all legal. One thing you learn in a place like Pelican Roost is that aging does not always mean maturing. Sometimes it goes the opposite way, like this guy.

WOMAN exits. MAN enters.

MAN:
I SAW NORMA JEAN GO IN THE WELLNESS ROOM.
THAT'S WHERE THEY CHECK CHOLESTEROL.
SO I HIT "GO" ON MY HOVEROUND.
I PARKED IT IN THE VERY NEXT STALL.
I STUCK MY ARM IN THE CUFF OF THE PRESSURE MACHINE.
I ASKED HER IF SHE'D LIKE TO GET A BITE.
SHE LOOKED AT ME THROUGH HER TRIFOCALED EYES
AND SAID THAT YES, THAT SHE JUST MIGHT.

"COME ON BACK TO MY ROOM," SHE SAID.
"I GOT CRACKERS AND SOME MARMALADE."
SO I FOLLOWED HER DOWN THE HALLWAY
PAST THE SECOND FLOOR PROMENADE.
BUT THEN MY SCOOTER FELL BEHIND.
I'D RUN IT OUT OF JUICE.
SO I CRAWLED BEHIND HER DOWN THE HALLWAY
AS I SANG TO HER CABOOSE.

+ WOMAN (OFFSTAGE):
HELP!

SFX: COWBELL

I'VE FALLEN FOR YOU
AND I CAN'T GET UP.
I CAN'T UNDERSTAND IT
ALL OF MY LIFE
I'VE BEEN A STUD
NOW,
MY MOJO AIN'T WORKIN'
AND I'M A DUD
HELP!

SFX: COWBELL

MAN + (OFFSTAGE) WOMAN (CONT'D):
    I'VE FALLEN FOR YOU
    AND I CAN'T GET UP.

MAN:
    TWIN SISTERS NAMED PEARL AND OLIVE
    THE HOTTEST BABES A MAN COULD EVER MEET.
    THEY WERE ALWAYS ASKIN' THE OTHER GUYS
    IF THEY'D LIKE TO GO BACK TO THEIR SUITE.
    I TRIED AND I TRIED BUT WHENEVER THEY SPIED ME
    THEY'D TURN AND SHUFFLE OFF THE OTHER WAY.
    SO I CORNERED PEARL AND OLIVE.
    AND ASKED THEM WHAT THE OTHER GUYS HAD, PER SE.
    OLIVE LOOKED AT PEARL AND PEARL LOOKED AT OLIVE
    THEN BOTH OF THEM LOOKED BACK AT ME.
    "IT'S NOT THAT WE DON'T LIKE YOU," SAID PEARL
    "IT'S OUR REPUTATIONS, YOU SEE."
    "WE LIMIT OUR GUESTS," OLIVE SAID
    "WE ONLY ASK ALZHEIMER'S MEN.
    CUZ AFTER THEY LEAVE OUR PLACE AT NIGHT,
    NONE OF THEM REMEMBERS WHERE HE'S BEEN."

MAN (ONSTAGE) & WOMAN (OFFSTAGE):
    HELP!

SFX: COWBELL

    I'VE FALLEN FOR YOU
    AND I CAN'T GET UP.
    I CAN'T UNDERSTAND IT
    ALL OF MY LIFE
    I'VE BEEN A STUD
    NOW,
    MY MOJO AIN'T WORKIN'
    AND I'M A DUD
    HELP!

SFX: COWBELL

    I'VE FALLEN FOR YOU
    AND I CAN'T GET UP.

SFX: COWBELL

    MAN exits.

SCENE 3

IT'S A WONDERFUL PLACE

NAOMI *(entering)*: Hi there and welcome to Pelican Roost, or as my kids call it "Pelican's Last Roost." I'm Naomi Lipschitz-Yamamoto-Murphy. Realtor. Not only do I live here, I sell here.

My kids— when they dropped me off here— well, their little evil hearts were in the right place— as they shoved me outta the back door of their Subaru, I said "Why?" They said to me, "MA, what if you should become bedridden?" Bedridden? I haven't been bedridden since Mr. Lipschitz passed away.

But hey, Pelican Roost? It's a wonderful place!

They feed me, they make my bed, they take me on bus tours— It's just like a cruise— but the final destination is not the Bahamas.

But hey, Pelican Roost? It's a wonderful place!

Like the recreational activities. For people who are hard of hearing? There's the banjo bagpipe band. People with short-term memory problems? They listen to Rush Limbaugh. He makes sense to them. And for the incontinents? Water aerobics.

But hey, Pelican Roost? It's a wonderful place!

Except for the spa!

All those mirrors!

SCENE 4

SONG #3: MY HIDE

NAOMI:
SAGGIN', SAGGIN', SAGGIN'.
SAGGIN', SAGGIN', SAGGIN'.
SAGGIN', SAGGIN', SAGGIN'.
THOUGH MY TUSH IS DRAGGIN'
AND MY TITS ARE WAGGIN'

+ MAN (OFFSTAGE):
MY HIDE.

NAOMI:
IN MY ALL TOGETHER
I RESEMBLE LEATHER.
LOOKS LIKE I'VE BEEN IN FORMALDEHYDE.
IT'S BECOMING URGEN'.
I NEED A PLASTIC SURGEON.
AN ACRE OF SKIN TO SUBDIVIDE.

+ MAN (OFFSTAGE):
NIP IT UP, CUT IT OFF,
CUT IT OFF, NIP IT UP.
NIP IT UP, CUT IT OFF
MY HIDE.
NIP IT UP, CUT IT OFF,
CUT IT OFF, NIP IT UP.
NIP IT UP, CUT IT OFF,
MY HIDE.

NAOMI:
SAGGIN', SAGGIN', SAGGIN'.
SAGGIN', SAGGIN', SAGGIN'.
SAGGIN', SAGGIN', SAGGIN'.
THEY CAN FIX MY WAGON
AND MY SADDLEBAG IN

+ MAN (OFFSTAGE):
MY HIDE.

NAOMI:
BOTOXED AND LIPOSUCT-ED.
STRETCHED AND TUMMY TUCK-ED.
THE ONLY THING THAT'S LOOSE IS WHAT'S INSIDE.
WHEN I'M PUSHING EIGHTY AND LOOK ACETATE-Y
I'LL BE SUSPICIOUSLY WIDE-EYED.

MAN (OFFSTAGE):
> SHOOT IT UP, SUCK IT OUT.
> SUCK IT OUT, SHOOT IT UP.
> SHOOT IT UP, SUCK IT OUT.

BOTH:
> MY HIDE.
>
> SHOOT IT UP, SUCK IT OUT.
> SUCK IT OUT, SHOOT IT UP.
> SHOOT IT UP, SUCK IT OUT.
> MY HIDE.
>
> NIP IT UP, CUT IT OFF.
> CUT IT OFF, NIP IT UP.
> NIP IT UP, CUT IT OFF
> MY HIDE.
>
> SHOOT IT UP, SUCK IT OUT.
> SUCK IT OUT, SHOOT IT UP.
> SHOOT IT UP, SUCK IT OUT
> MY HIDE.
>
> NIP IT UP, CUT IT OFF.
> CUT IT OFF, NIP IT UP.
> NIP IT UP, CUT IT OFF
> MY HIDE.

NAOMI:
> NIP IT UP, CUT IT OFF MY HIDE!

NAOMI exits.

SCENE 5

SONG #4: LOST-MY-DENTURES-ON-STEAK-NIGHT BLUES

HUNGRY MAN enters.

HUNGRY MAN:
MONDAY NIGHT IS PASTA.
TUESDAY NIGHT SOUFFLÉ.
WEDNESDAY NIGHT LASAGNA.
THURSDAY CONSOMMÉ.
FRIDAY NIGHT IS OYSTER STEW.

HUNGRY MAN:
SATURDAY CHEESE FONDUE.
BUT SUNDAY NIGHT IS STEAK NIGHT
AND THERE'S NO WAY I CAN CHEW.

HUNGRY MAN & WOMAN (OFFSTAGE):
SUNDAY NIGHT IS STEAK NIGHT.
AND MY TEETH HAVE DISAPPEARED.
I'VE LOOKED IN EVERY CLOSET,
EVERY DRAWER AND EVEN IN THE CHANDELIER.

HUNGRY MAN: They're not here.

(Singing)
THINGS ARE BAD, IT'S CERTAIN.
WHENEVER I SPEAK I SPIT.
MY ONCE PROUD CHIN IS SUNKEN IN.
MY MOUTH LOOKS LIKE A PIT.
MY SOCIAL LIFE IS HURTIN'.
AND THE WIFE DON'T WANNA KISS.
WELL, IT'S NOT THAT SHE DON'T WANNA,
SHE JUST CAN'T FIND MY LIPS!

HUNGRY MAN & WOMAN (OFFSTAGE):
SUNDAY NIGHT IS STEAK NIGHT
AND MY TEETH HAVE GONE AWAY.
I WOULDN'T GIVE A DAMN
IF THIS WERE ANY OTHER DAY
I'D GET ANOTHER SET
IF ONLY MEDICARE WOULD PAY.

HUNGRY MAN: Oatmeal tonight!

HUNGRY MAN exits.

SCENE 6

INTERNET CLASS

COMPUTER WOMAN *(entering)*: Hello, and welcome to The Pelican Rooster Computer Center. Now, all of Pelican Roost has been wired for Wi-Fi so we can be online all the time.

Now, when we're online, we need to know the acronyms, what all the little abbreviations mean. Who out there knows— OMG? OMG? *(Audience responds)* That's right— Oh My God.

And how bout the FAQs— the FAQs? Yes! the Frequently Asked Questions.

OK... AFK? AFK? Anyone? AFK means "Away From Keyboard."

And CYA? CYA? *(Audience responds)* "Cover Your Ass?" No— but you must work for [insert name of a disgraced politician]. No. CYA means "See Ya"— See Ya! You have been sending entirely the wrong message.

Then there's LOL. *(Audience responds)* That's right! Laugh out loud.

We use the computers for everything. For email, for shopping and even for... online dating.

I tried it once.

SCENE 7

SONG #5: WALKERDUDE@FACEBOOK DOT COM

COMPUTER WOMAN:
I WENT ONLINE LOOKING FOR
SOMEONE WHO WOULDN'T BORE
ME TO TEARS AND IF HE
COULD E-MAIL ME
AND SEND IT A-S-A-P.
I FOUND HIM— O-M-G!
HE'S WALKERDUDE AT FACEBOOK DOT COM.

THE FIRST TIME HE WROTE ME
HE SAID THAT HE HOPED WE
WOULD WRITE EVERY NIGHT AND DAY,
THOUGH HE WAS A-F-K,
GETTING A HIP X-RAY.
I SIGNED OFF "C-Y-A."
WALKERDUDE AT FACEBOOK DOT COM.

HE ASKED ME THE F-A-Q.
WHAT DID I LIKE TO DO?
I TOLD HIM DANCING
AND MIDDAY ROMANCING.
A MAN WITH ENDURANCE
AND PRIVATE INSURANCE.
WALKERDUDE AT FACEBOOK DOT COM.

OUR LOVE WAS SWELLING,
WE WERE L-O-L-ING.
THERE WAS NO NEED FOR SPELLING U-C
I LOVED LIKE A LEMMING
WE WERE ALWAYS I-M-ING
TILL ONE DAY HE SAID
THAT HE'D "B-R-B."
(Speaking)
Be right back. But he wasn't.
(Singing)
I CHECKED IN AT MYSPACE,
THEN BACK TO FACE—

COMPUTER WOMAN (CONT'D):
    BOOK AND EACH CYBER NOOK
    AND PATH THAT HE MIGHT HAVE TOOK
    LOOKING FOR ME
    WORE OUT THE ENTER KEY
    WALKERDUDE AT FACEBOOK DOT COM.

    I'VE WIDENED MY SETTINGS
    FOR SECURITY GETTING
    A MUCH LARGER CACHE
    AND SPAM FOLDER STASH
    I'VE QUIT CYBER-DATING
    BUT I'LL ALWAYS BE WAITING FOR
    WALKERDUDE AT FACEBOOK DOT COM.
    WALKERDUDE AT FACEBOOK DOT COM.

           COMPUTER WOMAN exits.

SCENE 8

LAWYER enters with music.

Speeches are punctuated by chords and runs notated by(^) symbol.

LAWYER: You can trust me, cuz I'm(^) a lawyer(^).

Are you a "mature" man or woman?(^) Do you wake up every morning with the aches(^) and pains(^) that can only be attributed to the aging process?(^)

Someone is responsible for you waking up each morning(^) and they should pay.(^) This specialized field is called(^) "Extended Life Liability."(^)

We've found that the makers of vitamins(^) and supplements,(^) the owners of gyms and spas,(^) and yes, the medical establishment itself,(^) they have all conspired to make you live longer.(^) And they should pay.(^)

If you are alive,(^) or think you may be alive in the future,(^) call me(^) at 666-LAWYERS.(^) That's 666-L-A-W-Y-E-R-Z.

And remember, you can trust me, cuz I'm(^) a lawyer.(^)

Thank you!

LAWYER exits.

SCENE 9

SONG #7: THE ORGAN DONOR SONG

NURSE *(entering)*: Welcome to the Pelican Roost Wellness Center. And now, the Wellness Center question of the day...

How can you combine healthy living with extreme recycling? We have a prescription for that. "When you're done with it, let someone else run with it."

(Singing)

IF YOUR CAR BREAKS DOWN, YOU GET TOWED TO TOWN

THEY REPLACE YOUR RADIATOR.

YOUR TV QUITS, YOUR PHONE'S ON THE FRITZ,

DROP IT OFF AND PICK IT UP LATER.

IF YOUR KIDNEYS GET WEAK OR YOUR LUNGS START TO LEAK

IF YOUR EYES NEED A ROD OR A CONER.

YOU'LL WANT SOME SPARES, SO DO WHAT'S FAIR. BE AN ORGAN DONOR.

DOCTOR enters with box of organs.

DOCTOR: Here's today's delivery, Nurse.

NURSE: Thank you, Doctor!

NURSE & DOCTOR *(putting on gloves)*:

ORGAN DONOR, ORGAN DONOR.

NO NEED FOR YOU TO BE THE FINAL OWNER,

OF YOUR OLD SPARE PARTS, YOUR JOIE D'VIE.

NURSE:

DON'T KEEP THE STUFF THAT YOU DON'T NEED.

NURSE & DOCTOR:

ORGAN DONOR, ORGAN DONOR.

LEAVE YOUR PILES TO GOOD OLD GOMER.

LEAVE YOUR LUNGS, LIVER, LONGEVITY.

JOIN THE ORGAN DONOR FAM'LY!

NURSE explores organ box.

DOCTOR:

YOU'LL BE FINE, PUT YOUR NAME ON THE LINE

GIVE AWAY A PIECE OF YOURSELF.

YOU MAY BE GONE, BUT THE PARTY ROCKS ON,

YOU'LL KEEP ANOTHER BUDDY OFF THE SHELF.

YOUR LAST GOOD DEED. YOU WON'T BLEED. HIT A GRAND SLAM HOMER.

SIGN UP TODAY, GIVE IT AWAY. BE AN ORGAN DONOR.

NURSE: Doctor. I think we have a complete body here!

DOCTOR: Yes, Nurse. And a vacancy in room 314.

NURSE & DOCTOR:
ORGAN DONOR, ORGAN DONOR.
NO NEED FOR YOU TO BE THE FINAL OWNER,
OF YOUR OLD SPARE PARTS, YOUR VIRILITY.

NURSE:
DON'T KEEP THE STUFF THAT YOU DON'T NEED.

NURSE & DOCTOR:
ORGAN DONOR, ORGAN DONOR.
MINE GETS BROKE, I'LL NEED A LOANER.
THE ONLY THING YOU CAN'T LEAVE IS YOUR SANITY.
JOIN THE ORGAN DONOR...
ORGAN DONOR...!
ORGAN DONOR FAM'LY!

DOCTOR exits.

SCENE 10

COMEDY HOUR

NURSE: Lucky, lucky you. Because right now, it's Comedy Hour here in our Kumbaya Community Room. This week, like last week, and the week before, we have a resident Rooster, a real fixture in our hallways. No, he's not the Purell dispenser. He won the 1962 Rodney Dangerfield Award as the comedian least likely to earn respect. And he is the only comedian to actually kill a cat in the Catskills.

Ladies and gentlemen— originally from Poughkeepsie-By-The-Sea, please welcome Pelican Roost's answer to Ambien. Mister Ben Younger!

NURSE exits as BEN YOUNGER enters.

BEN YOUNGER: Hya doin' Hya doin' Hya doin'! *(To aud member)* Hey, remember me? From last week? You don't? I love workin' the Memory Unit!

Me and my wife, 'bout five years ago, we moved into Pelican Roost. We had to cuz I had fallen down. Immediately they put me into a yoga class. They said it would be good for my balance. An hour the first day, standing on one foot then the other. Then, I went back to my room, checked my bank book, and it didn't do any good. My balance was the same.

SFX: OFFSTAGE VIBRASLAP

What? Ya never been to the Catskills?

Me and my wife, 'bout five years ago, we moved into Pelican Roost. We took an airplane down here and the security was terrible. We put our luggage up on the conveyer belt. It goes through the machine and I walk through the metal detector. There, the guard stops me and says "Mr. Younger, I hafta search your bag." I said, "That's no bag, that's my wife!"

SFX: OFFSTAGE VIBRASLAP

What? Ya never been to the Catskills?

The guard, he made me late for my flight. And I had to go to the bathroom. I think I could go before I go to the gate, but no. The wife says hurry up. I think I could go when I get to the gate, but no. Hurry up and get on the plane. I think I can go when I get on the plane but no, sit down, buckle your seat belt. I sit down. I buckle my seat belt. Finally the plane takes off. Finally we get to cruising altitude. Finally the pilot comes on and says "Feel free to walk about the cabin." I unbuckle my seat belt. I stand up. I walk down the aisle. I open the lavatory door. But no, I'm stymied again! There's a sign over the toilet. It says "No Foreign Objects In The Toilet." Last night— I'd eaten Chinese.

SFX: OFFSTAGE VIBRASLAP

BEN YOUNGER (CONT'D): What? Ya never been to the Catskills?

See ya next week, folks!

BEN YOUNGER exits.

SCENE 11

COUNTRY CLUB WOMAN enters on phone.

COUNTRY CLUB WOMAN: Yes, Muffy. I don't know what to do with him. Since he retired, he is home all the time. Last week he tried to teach me how to run the dishwasher. What's next? How to match his socks? Well, I just picked up a brochure. Pelican Roost has an election coming up! For the board of directors of the Pelican Roost Home Owners Association. I think it's just the thing he needs. I'm going to tell him just as soon as he comes home.

COUNTRY CLUB MAN *(entering):* Honey, I'm home.

COUNTRY CLUB WOMAN: He's home. Bye. *(To Country Club Man)* Dear, we have an election coming up. You could sign up today to run for the board of directors of The Pelican Roost Home Owners Association!

COUNTRY CLUB MAN:
IT SOUNDS LIKE FUN; I'LL BE THE ONE MY NEIGHBORS WILL ELECT
A PILLAR OF MY COMMUNITY THIS PLACE I WILL DIRECT
A MEETING ONCE OR TWICE A MONTH AND THE CLUB BAR TO INSPECT
I'M GONNA BE A MEMBER OF MY OWNERS' ASSOCIATION

COUNTRY CLUB WOMAN:
HE'S GONNA TO BE A MEMBER OF THE OWNERS' ASSOCIATION
> *(Speaking)*

Maybe, just maybe you could be president.

COUNTRY CLUB MAN: President? Really? Do you think so?

COUNTRY CLUB WOMAN: Of course dear. Then I'll be the first lady!

COUNTRY CLUB MAN:
THE CAMPAIGN IS A HAPPY TIME I'M GOIN' DOOR TO DOOR
I'M PROMISING THEM EVERYTHING FROM THE CEILING TO THE FLOOR
MORE SERVICES MORE PERKS MORE DISCOUNTS ON THE COURSE
PLEASE VOTE FOR ME FOR PRESIDENT OF THE OWNERS' ASSOCIATION.

COUNTRY CLUB WOMAN:
VOTE FOR HIM FOR PRESIDENT OF THE OWNERS' ASSOCIATION.
AND THEN THE DAY HAS COME.
THE COUNT IS MADE THE RACE IS DONE.

COUNTRY CLUB MAN *(into phone):* Hello? Yes. Really? *(To wife)* I won! I won! I'm President of the Pelican Roost Homeowners' Association!

COUNTRY CLUB WOMAN:
IT WASN'T HARD: NO ONE ELSE HAD RUN!
> *(Speaking)*

That night he took me to the club to celebrate.

COUNTRY CLUB MAN: Thank you for your vote.

COUNTRY CLUB WOMAN: He went from table to table—

COUNTRY CLUB MAN: I'm honored.

COUNTRY CLUB WOMAN: —glad-handing and buying drinks for everyone.

COUNTRY CLUB MAN: Happy to represent you.

COUNTRY CLUB WOMAN: And to every single person he said:

COUNTRY CLUB MAN *(while Woman mouths it)*: If you ever need anything... anything at all... just call me.

COUNTRY CLUB WOMAN: Well...

SFX: PHONE RINGS

(Singing)
THE CALLS THEY STARTED COMING IN THE VERY NEXT A-M
COUNTRY CLUB MAN:
ONE MAN'S LIGHT WAS SHINING OUT
WHILE ANOTHER'S WAS SHINING IN
THEY MOW THE GRASS TOO EARLY,
THEY MOW THE GRASS TOO LATE
THAT'S WHY THEY CALL
THE PRESIDENT OF THE OWNERS' ASSOCIATION.
COUNTRY CLUB WOMAN:
THAT'S WHY THEY CALL
THE PRESIDENT OF THE OWNERS' ASSOCIATION.

SFX: PHONE RINGS

(Speaking)
Hello? It's for you.

COUNTRY CLUB MAN:
ONE OWNER'S DOG HAD GOTTEN OUT AND POOPED UPON THE WALK
OF 14-C WHO'S CALLING ME BECAUSE SHE WANTS TO TALK.
THE SWIMMING POOL IS TURNING GREEN; THE BAR IS OUT OF GIN.
AND WHO DO THEY CALL?
THE PRESIDENT OF THE OWNERS' ASSOCIATION.
COUNTRY CLUB WOMAN:
THEY CALL AND CALL
THE PRESIDENT OF THE OWNERS' ASSOCIATION.

SFX: PHONE RINGS

COUNTRY CLUB MAN: Hello? Yes, this is the president of the homeowners association. The white paint on your ceiling doesn't match the brochure? Well, sir, I'll send a new brochure right over.

SFX: PHONE RINGS

COUNTRY CLUB MAN: Hello? Yes, this is the president of the homeowners associa... No, Madam, I will not help you take off your support hose!

SFX: PHONE RINGS

Hello? Yes, this is the president of the homeowners asso... Children?!? *(Mockingly)* CHILDREN??? Laughing and playing across the street? How dare they! I suggest, madam, you lure them into your gingerbread house and pop them into your oven! I quit!

COUNTRY CLUB WOMAN: But you can't dear. Not till the end of your term! Another two years.

COUNTRY CLUB MAN:
LOCK THE DOOR AND DRAW THE BLINDS,
DON'T LET 'EM KNOW WE'RE HOME.
STAY INSIDE, TURN OUT THE LIGHTS

SFX: PHONE RINGS

AND DON'T PICK UP THE PHONE.
WE'LL CHANGE OUR NAMES. WE'LL MOVE TO FRANCE.

COUNTRY CLUB WOMAN: Oui!

COUNTRY CLUB MAN: Yes, both of us.

(Singing)
NO ONE WILL EVER KNOW
I WAS ONCE THE PRESIDENT OF THE OWNERS' ASSOCIATION.

COUNTRY CLUB WOMAN:
HE IS STILL THE PRESIDENT OF THE OWNERS' ASSOCIATION.

COUNTRY CLUB MAN: And God help anyone

BOTH:
WHOEVER BECOMES PRESIDENT OF THE OWNERS' ASSOCI...

SFX: PHONE RINGS

(Speaking)
Arghhhhhhh!

BOTH exit screaming.

SCENE 12

WALKER MAN and WALKER WOMAN enter.

WALKER MAN & WALKER WOMAN:
DO-WALK DO-WALK DO-WALK DO-WALK
DO-WALK DO-WALK DO-WALK

HOW WE LOVE OUR WALKERS,
CHROME AND SHINY STEEL.
HOW WE LOVE OUR WALKERS,
SENIOR PIMP MOBILES.
CARRESSING THE HANDRAILS
AND SLIDING OUR BALLS TO GET AROUND.
WE WON'T FALL DOWN

WALKER MAN:
NOW I HAVE MY FREEDOM EVEN ON THE COURSE.
MY GOLF CART AND MY WALKER ARE NOW A DRIVING FORCE.
I HIT IT SO FAR, I'M SHOOTING NEAR PAR, SEVENTY-FOUR.

WALKER WOMAN: He cheats on his score.

　　　(Singing)
NOW I HAVE MY FREEDOM ALWAYS HERE WITH ME.
WHEN I'M AT THE MARKET AND WHEN I HAVE TO PEE.
YOU CAN SEE ME COMIN' CUZ I DECORATE THIS RACK
WITH FLASHING LIGHTS, A SIREN AND A LITHIUM BATTERY PACK.
DO-WALK DO-WALK DO-WALK DO-WALK

WALKER MAN & WALKER WOMAN:
HOW WE LOVE OUR WALKERS,
CHROME AND SHINY STEEL.
HOW WE LOVE OUR WALKERS,
SENIOR PIMP MOBILES.

WALKER MAN & WALKER WOMAN:
WE'RE NEVER PRONE, WE'RE OUT ON OUR OWN, ON OUR WALKERS,
OUT ON OUR OWN
BEEP, BEEP, BEEP, BEEP, BEEP, BEEP, BEEP.

WALKER MAN & WALKER WOMAN:
WE'RE MOBILE.

WALKER WOMAN exits.

SCENE 13

SONG #10: GOLF CART SEDUCTION

>*During musical interlude, WALKER MAN changes onstage a-
>la stripper into SLEAZY MAN.*

SLEAZY MAN: Hey, baby. After a long evening— happy hour drinks— early bird dinner— concert on the lawn— when the day gets late, 5 or 5:30, my mind turns to the finer things in life— like a ride in my golf cart. My golf cart— custom-styled with the fins of a 1963 Cadillac. Tuck and rolled seats to caress me. And fringe around the top that plays in the breeze like the pleats in a cheerleader's skirt. And the seats recline— all the way back, for those quiet moments when we get the urge— for a nap.

>*(Singing)*
>NOW EVERYTHING IS SWELL WHEN YOU'RE IN PELICAN ROOST
>DRIVIN' MY CART, I'M AN ACE IN A DEUCE.
>IF I SEE YOU ON THE CART PATH, I'LL BLOW YA A TOOT.
>'CAUSE EVERYTHING IS SWELL AGAIN,
>I WON'T KISS AND TELL AGAIN,
>YOU CAN SMELL THAT NEW CART SMELL AGAIN
>AT PELICAN ROOST!
>*(Speaking)*

I'll be your designated driver, baby.

>*SLEAZY MAN exits.*

SCENE 14

ROOMS

NAOMI enters.

NAOMI: Hi there. Remember me? I'm Naomi Lipschitz-Yamamoto-Murphy. Realtor. And not only do I live here, I sell here. We got four different kinds of homes here at Pelican Roost. I myself have lived in three of 'em. So Far.

The first was a studio. I lived there with Mr. Lipschitz.

The studio has one bathroom, which, as you can imagine, was a problem for Mr. Lipschitz and myself. One morning I found myself brushin' my teeth with his Preparation H. But, hey, they're beautiful units.

Unfortunately, Mr. Lipschitz passed away, so I upgraded— to Mr. Yamamoto, and his one-bedroom. The one bedroom was nice, but noisy! Burt and Alice, our upstairs neighbors— every night! Burt took those Cialis pills, and we didn't have to see Alice, we could hear Alice. But, hey, they're beautiful units.

Unfortunately, Mr. Yamamoto passed away, so I upgraded— to Mr. Murphy, and his two-bedroom. Now, the two-bedroom has two-and-a-half bathrooms. We use the half-bath to store the Readers Digests. But, hey they're beautiful units.

Hmmmm... I wonder how Mr. Murphy's doin'? Ya never know— it maybe time to upgrade to—

SCENE 15

NAOMI:
OUR GOLF-CART COMMUNITY, NOT TOO FAR BACK
PARK OUT IN FRONT, NEAR THE GOLF CART TRACK
ALOHA, VELL-COOM, CIAO, AND SHALOM
IT'S YOUR SENIOR RESORT-STYLE HOME

WE'VE DESIGNED IT TO LOOK LIKE A TROPICAL ISLE
MAHOGANY HANDRAILS WITH NON-SLIP TILE
EACH PALM TREE'S EQUIPPED WITH A 911 PHONE
IT'S YOUR SENIOR RESORT-STYLE HOME

EVERY THURSDAY AT 4 THERE'S A GOLF CART PARADE
AND SOME VETERANS REINACT THE CUBAN BLOCKADE
(Speaking)

This place that I'm sellin' ya, Pelican Roost, is more than just bricks and mortar and former husbands. It's a lifestyle. I never had one of those before. Before I settled here, I looked at Pelican Island, Pelican Marsh, Pelican Nest, Pelican Perch, Pelican Place, Pelican Preserve, and then after a piece of pelican pie at The Rusty Pelican, I found Pelican Roost, and hey, they're beautiful units. Why, even the defibrillators look like pelicans.

(Singing)
IF YOU'RE CLEVER YOU CAN CHARGE UP YOUR GOLF CART FOR FREE,
WITH THE POWER CORD RUN TO YOUR NEIGHBOR'S AC.
SIGN ON THE LINE, WE'LL FLOAT YOU A LOAN
ON YOUR SENIOR RESORT-STYLE HOME.
(Speaking)

Not only do I sell here, I live here.

(Singing)
BUY A SENIOR RESORT-STYLE HOME.

NAOMI exits.

SCENE 16

LAWYER enters with music.

Speeches are punctuated by chords and runs notated by(^) symbol.

LAWYER: You can trust me, cuz I'm a(^) lawyer.(^) Are you a mature man or woman?(^)

Sometimes as we mature, we may suffer injuries.(^)

And sometimes as we mature even more, we may not remember we have suffered an injury.(^) I believe that you should not have to remember, to collect fair compensation.(^) I call this specialized field of practice(^) "Injury Remembrance."(^)

If you don't remember being injured,(^) call 666-LAWYERS.(^)

That's 666-L-A-W-Y-E-R-Z.

And remember, you can trust me cuz I'm(^) a lawyer.(^)

Thank you!

LAWYER exits.

SCENE 17

NURSE enters.

NURSE:
> NOW EVERYTHING IS SWELL WHEN YOU'RE IN PELICAN ROOST
> NO MATTER HOW YOUR DOIN' WE'LL GIVE YA A BOOST
> *(Speaking)*

Ah, the Wellness Center, where we educate, medicate and lubricate. Planning a night out with new friends? We have a prescription for that. "It's OK to get close, but don't get something gross."

> *(Singing)*
> VERNON FELT A BURNIN' IN A VERY PRIVATE PLACE.
> IT REALLY MADE HIM NERVOUS
> CUZ HE'D SPENT THE NIGHT WITH GRACE.
> JUST TWO NIGHTS BEFORE THAT,
> GRACE HAD BEEN WITH BILL.
> BILL WAS DOIN' MYRTLE,
> AND MYRTLE DOIN' PHIL.
> PHIL WAS AMBIDEXTROUS, HE WAS SHTUPPING JANE AND STU.
> AT DIFFERENT TIMES OF COURSE.
> AND THEY'D BEEN BUSY, TOO.
> VERNON PASSED THE WORD, HE SAID THEY SHOULD BE SEEN.
> AND WHEN THE BLOOD WORK CAME BACK, THEY ALL TESTED CLEAN
> CUZ EVERYTHING IS SWELL WHEN YOU'RE IN PELICAN ROOST

IM-PATIENT MAN (OFFSTAGE): Nurse! Nurse!

> *(Singing)*
> NO MATTER HOW YOU'RE DOIN' WE'LL GIVE YA A BOOST

IM-PATIENT MAN enters.

> *(Speaking)*

 Nurse! Nurse!

NURSE:
> GOLF CARTS AND HOOK-UPS ALWAYS SUMPTHIN' TO DO

IM-PATIENT MAN: But I'm sick!

NURSE:
> WE HAVE EVERYTHING YOU WANT HERE AND IT'S WAITING FOR YOU.

IM-PATIENT MAN: But Nurse!

NURSE: You look fine. I told you that yesterday, and the day before, and the day before that, and the day before the day before...

SCENE 18

SONG #14: HYPOCHONDRIACAL

IM-PATIENT MAN:
> I MAY LOOK QUITE HEALTHY
> BUT THE END, IT CAN BE STEALTHY.
> I AM SICK.

NURSE: But the doctor told you...

IM-PATIENT MAN:
> THOUGH THE DOCTOR FINDS ME WELL,
> THIS MAY BE THE FINAL KNELL.
> I'M GOIN' QUICK.

NURSE: You're just imagining these symptoms.

IM-PATIENT MAN:
> SEE WHERE I GOT MALARIA?
> BUT THE DOCTOR DOESN'T CARE, YA
> HAVE TO DIE AND THEN THEY'LL BUR'YA
> RIGHT THERE IN HIS WAITING AREA.
> BEFORE HE FINDS HE'S WRONG,
> I COULD BE LONG GONE.
> I AM SICK.

NURSE *(exiting):* I'll see if the Doctor will see you!

IM-PATIENT MAN:
> LAST NIGHT I HAD A DREAM-A
> I'D CONTRACTED EMPHYSEMA
> AND THE RUNS.
> AND THE COUGH I HAD THIS MORNING,
> COULD IT BE THE EARLY WARNING
> OF BLACK LUNG?
>
> AND THE BLURRING OF MY SIGHT,
> DON'T YOU THINK THAT I JUST MIGHT
> HAVE A LATENT STIGMATISM,
> FROM A BURSTING ANEURYSM
> SEE THIS RASH ON MY SKIN?
> MY TOES ARE POINTING IN!
> I AM SICK.

IM-PATIENT MAN (CONT'D):
    ADIOS! AFTER I'M TOAST,
    I'LL COME BACK AS A GHOST
    I'LL HAUNT H-M-OS
    I COULD BE THE FIRST TO DIE
    FROM A STY IN MY EYE.
    IS THIS PINK?
    WILL I SUFFER AS I LINGER
    FROM THIS HANGNAIL ON MY FINGER
    DO YA THINK?

    COULD A GERM OR PARASITE,
    AS IT SWIMS WITH ALL ITS MIGHT
    THROUGH MY VEINS AND ARTERIES,
    CAUSE MY BLEEDING HEART TO SEIZE?
    IT WOULD BE IRONIC TO DIE FROM MY COLONIC.
    I AM SICK.

    LOTS'A FIBER I'M CONSUMIN'
    BUT THERE'S BLOATIN' AND THERE'S BOOMIN'.
    I'M NOT WELL.
    I PUT SUNSCREEN ON MY SKIN.
    SUPPLEMENTS I'M TAKIN' IN.
    THEY TASTE LIKE HELL.

    ORGANIC MILK AND JUICE,
    COULD THEY BE ANOTHER NOOSE?
    CUZ THEY HAVEN'T BEEN INSPECTED
    BY THE PEOPLE WE ELECTED
    TO THE F-D-A AND OSHA.
    PERHAPS I SHOULD TRY KOSHA'.
    I AM SICK.

    ADIEU!
    IT'S PNEUMONIA AND FLU!
    A-A-A-CHOO!
    DID I GET IT ON YOU?
        (Speaking)
  I'm terribly sorry but you see...

IM-PATIENT MAN (CONT'D):
> I AM LYING ON MY DEATHBED
> FROM THIS PIMPLE ON MY FOREHEAD
> AND I PRAY
> THAT THE GOOD LORD HE WILL SPARE ME.
> I AM SURE THAT HE WILL DARE ME
> CHANGE MY WAYS.
> I'VE STOPPED SMOKING,
> I'VE STOPPED DRINKING,
> BUT I CANNOT STOP A-THINKING
>
> EVERY TIC AND EVERY TWITCH
> WILL SEND ME TO THE DITCH.
>
> DRESS ME UP IN MY BLACK TIE
> AND KISS MY ASS GOODBYE.
>
> GOTTA CHECK MY BEEPER,
> I'M EXPECTING THE GRIM REAPER.
>
> I'M SCHEDULED TO BURN
> SO ENGRAVE THIS ON MY URN
>
> HE WAS SICK. I AM SICK.
> I'LL COME BACK TOMORROW!

IM-PATIENT MAN exits.

SCENE 19

THE BATTLE OF ROOM 109

POETRY WOMAN enters with large book. She notices stool (swivel) on stage, walks over and pulls it over to stage center.

Take your time. She gets up on stool— backwards! She swivels around on the stool several times, enjoying the ride and the audience response. She gets her other leg up on the stool.

POETRY WOMAN: And now it's time for the Pelican Roost Poetry Corner. Today we feature "The Battle of Room 109" written by... well, I wrote it!

Four of us lived in Building Seven,
All lined up, waiting for heaven.
Each room small and tidy with just enough sun. The rooms were alike.
All, save one.

Room 109, at the end of the hall,
Was a beautiful place, enough room for a ball.
Patio windows looked o'er lake and tee.
It was suddenly vacant and we all wanted the key.

There was Old Lady Springer in Room 106.
An indoor gardener with grow lights and sticks.
Heavy drapes on her windows, the thermostat hot.
She had too many plants. Move? I think not.

But McCracken, the gnome, sucking O-2,
He wanted that room, and who knew what he'd do?
In the past he'd bribed managers and room committee heads.
He'd sell his own mother, if she weren't dead.

Helen Highwater was an ex-army nurse.
She'd spit, she'd fight, she'd foam, she'd curse,
Attila the Hun on a walker with wheels.
She'd run you down in the hallway, then brake with a squeal.

POETRY WOMAN (CONT'D): Who gets 109? We'd be out in the hall
For a meeting that ev'ning where the gavel would fall.
But my rivals for 109 I'd disable
With the twist of a dial and the snip of a cable.

On my way to the meeting, after dinner, at 4,
I ambushed McCracken coming out of his door.
"How ya doin', Cracker? What'dya say?"
He stuck out his hand and I pumped it away.

My other hand reached down for his bottle.
Unseen by him, I twisted the throttle
From fifty percent way down to point four.
That gnome would sleep soundly 'fore he got to the door.

Then Highwater and walker flew past like Ben Hur.
I leapt out of a doorway, a ninja-like blur.
As deft as a gymnast, as quick as thrombosis
With my pen knife I cut through her break cable hoses.

She went straight down the hall, unable to brake,
Right through the meeting and into the lake.
She was out of the picture, and McCracken was saggin'.
109 was mine! Mine for the snaggin'!

Behind me I heard from the end of the hall
That gardener Springer and I heard her call.
"Are you coming to hear about my good news?
I'm leaving my old room. I'm making a move."

She said "My son, he's the manager here.
He got me these, isn't he dear?"
In her hand were the keys to room 109.
I couldn't believe it! It should have been mine!

POETRY WOMAN: The battle was over, but I've still got clout.

I'll use my last weapon to get Springer out.

I'll call the cops and give them a lead.

Cuz I've peeked in her room, she grows medical weed.

SCENE 20

EMERGENCY ANNOUNCEMENT

POETRY WOMAN (*goes to leaves but remembers*): Oh... yes! (*Rummages down her bra— coming up with note*) Attention! Roosters who use the parking garage. The owners of the 1982 blue Grand Marquis, the '87 Silver Town Car and the '76 Volvo station wagon with the Hubert Humphrey bumper sticker— this announcement is not for you. Everyone else? You've left your lights on— again.

Oh, there's more! A set of keys is missing— Nickolas Dent's Cadillac keys. We're concerned because, last time he drove, Mr. Dent misunderstood the term "drive-thru window." If you see him, get his keys.

POETRY WOMAN exits.

SCENE 21

SONG #15: A TON-AND-A-HALF OF CADILLAC STEEL

> *NICK DENT enters. He uses a combination of stools to create the illusion of driving a car.*

NICK DENT:

IT'S MAN'S MOST POWERFUL AUTOMOBILE,
A GIANT AUTOMOTIVE ON FOUR BIG WHEELS,
A TON-AND-A-HALF OF CADILLAC STEEL.
I'M NINETY-THREE AND I'M BEHIND THE WHEEL.

THE CIGARETTE LIGHTER HAS A SPECIAL PIN
WHERE I CAN PLUG MY PACEMAKER IN.
THE AIRBAGS HAVE AN OXYGEN PORT.
AN LS MODEL, IT STANDS FOR LIFE SUPPORT.

I'VE GOTTEN TOO SHORT TO SIT IN THE SEAT
TO SEE OVER THE DASH OR HIT THE BRAKES WITH MY FEET.
BUT THE DASH DOESN'T MATTER. IT'S NOT REALLY IN MY WAY.
I'M LEGALLY BLIND ANYWAY.

I'VE HIT LANDSCAPE MEDIANS AND STREET LIGHT POSTS.
I'VE TURNED SEVEN LITTLE PUPPIES INTO SEVEN LITTLE GHOSTS.
THERE'S A BICYCLE STICKIN' OUTTA MY CARBURATOR.
IT DON'T BOTHER ME NONE, I TAKE A MOOD ELEVATOR.

TO EV'RY PEDESTRIAN AND PARKING VALET,
IF YOU EVER SEE ME COMING, GET OUTTA THE WAY.
GRAMP'S IS GONNA GET YA FROM BEHIND THE WHEEL
OF MY 3000 POUNDS OF COUPE DE VILLE.
THAT'S A TON-AND-A-HALF OF CADILLAC STEEL.

> *(Speaking)*

Wanna ride?

> *Blackout.*
>
> *NICK DENT exits.*

SCENE 22

Lights up.

REAL ESTATE

NAOMI enters.

NAOMI: Hi there. Remember me? I'm Naomi Lipschitz-Yamamoto-Murphy. Realtor. And not only do I live here, I sell here. And my customers? Well, real estate isn't the only thing they're interested in gettin' their hands on— if ya know what I mean. You do know what I mean?

Last month, I had a guy come in, he was lookin' for something to appreciate— with someone to maintain his common areas. Appreciate? His common areas? But hey, I'm a professional. I showed him a house.

We found ourselves by the swimming pool. He asked if the pool was heated. I said, I didn't know. He then asked, in a husky voice, could he dip a toe? "Dip a toe?" My second husband Murray, Murray Yamamoto, may he rest in peace, was always wanting to "dip a toe." But I gotta tell ya, there's not enough Dr. Scholl's Foot Powder in the entire New York City Marathon to make me let him "dip a toe." Fannie Mae— but I won't. I got my common areas outta there.

He wanted me.

Then yesterday, I get a call from this French couple who wanted to see a condo in a newly erected high-rise. That's right, they started talking dirty right from the git-go.

I met 'em in the lobby and I walked into the elevator ahead of them. The man said to his wife what a lovely foyer I had. Now, I've always been aware of the magnetic properties of my foyer but really— in front of his wife? But hey, I'm a professional. I showed 'em a condo.

I unlocked the condo door. He took off for the kitchen and his wife turned to me and asked, in a husky voice, if I have a special place for her husband to put his Pinot Noir. His Pinot Noir?

I am about to tell her where her husband can put his Pinot Noir when the husband comes out saying he'd found the perfect place for the frommage. Frommage? Frommage a trois? I ran for the elevator. I heard them behind me say, "Wait, wait! We can all go down together." I pressed the close-door button— my foyer still intact. They wanted me.

Oh, look at the time. I gotta meet some Shriners. They say they want a new clubhouse but I think they just want to get me into the back of one of those little clown cars.

But hey, I'm a professional!

NAOMI exits.

SCENE 23

LEGAL KARMA

LAWYER enters with music.

Speeches are punctuated by chords and runs notated by(^) symbol.

LAWYER: You can trust me, cuz I'm a(^) lawyer.(^)

Are you a mature man or woman?(^)

Lawyers will promise mature men and women anything.(^) They will promise to get you money for the aches(^) and the pains(^) of living so long.(^) They will promise to get you money for injuries you do not remember,(^) but only I promise to get you money from lawyers who promise to get you money.(^) This specialized field is called(^) Karma.(^)

So, if you've ever called a lawyer,(^) Call me(^)— even if you've called me(^) at 666-LAWYERS.

That's 666-L-A-W-Y-E-R-Z.

You can trust me, cuz I'm(^) a lawyer.(^)

Thank you!

LAWYER exits.

SCENE 24

Happy Birthday underscore as WOMAN enters.

WOMAN: Oh, [PIANIST's name]. *(To audience)* Today's my birthday. *(Opening birthday cards)* Happy Birthday from [PIANIST's name]. Thank you, dear. Happy Birthday from the folks in the Wellness Center. Awww! Happy Birthday from Naomi. *(Pulls out thong panty)* I could never wear this.

Underscore.

(To audience)

But not for the reason you think.

(Singing)
WHEN I WAS YOUNG AND KINDA DUMB, I LISTENED TO A DARE.
MY FRIEND WOULD GET A TATTOO HERE IF I WOULD GET ONE THERE.
SHE SAID IT WOULD BE SEXY, AN APHRODESIAC.
TO GET A SKETCHING, SOMETHING FETCHING,
DOWN BELOW MY BACK.

+ MAN (OFFSTAGE) *(echoing)*:
TATTOO.
TATTOO.
TATTOO ON MY BUTT.

WOMAN:
THRU CATALOGS OF CATS AND DOGS,
PRETTY FLOWERS AND HEARTS
WE TRIED TO FIND FOR OUR BEHINDS
THE PERFECT WORKS OF ART.
MY FRIEND, SHE PICKED A TWINING VINE,
WITH LUSCIOUS GRAPES OF BLUE.
I CHOSE A LITTLE ROOSTER,
SAYING "COCK-A-DOODLE-DO."

+ MAN (OFFSTAGE) *(echoing)*:
TATTOO.
TATTOO.
TATTOO ON MY BUTT.

WOMAN:
THE TATTOO ARTIST SEEMED TO ME TO BE A LITTLE QUAINT.
HIS HEAD WAS BARE, A TATTOO THERE, A PORTRAIT OF A SAINT.
HE SAID, "THIS SAINT PROTECTS ME FROM THE TATTOO ARTIST'S HELL.
SHE HELPS ME GET THE PICTURES RIGHT, SHE EVEN HELPS ME SPELL."

WOMAN (CONT'D):
    WHEN HE FIN'LY FINISHED, I GOT TO TAKE A PEEK.
    I TWISTED LEFT SO I COULD CHECK. I GAZED UPON MY CHEEK.
    THE ROOSTER DIDN'T LOOK QUITE RIGHT, NO "COCK-A-DOODLE-DO."
    THE WORDS FROM OUT THE ROOSTER'S MOUTH
    SAID "ANY COCK'LL DO."

    I'VE TRIED
BOTH:
    SKIN GRAFTS,
    LASER BLASTS,
    DERMABRADE AND SUCH.
    CAN'T SOMEBODY HELP ME
    GET THIS TATTOO OFF MY BUTT?

    CLOSE YOUR EYES,
    CAUTERIZE,
    I'VE HAD IT LONG ENOUGH.
    IS THERE NOTHIN' I CAN DO
    TO GET THIS TATTOO OFF MY BUTT?
        (Echoing)
    TATTOO.
    TATTOO.
    TATTOO ON MY BUTT.
WOMAN: Oh what the hell!

        She grabs the thong.

SCENE 25

SONG #17: THE UPLIFTING VIAGRA MEDLEY

MAN enters.

MAN: Oh, honey. I have a little something for your birthday, too!

He hands WOMAN a pill bottle.

WOMAN & MAN:
HE CAN GET IT UP!
HE CAN GET IT UP!

*Simultaneously.

WOMAN*:
HE
CAN GET IT UP!

HE
CAN GET IT UP!

IN THE BEDROOM
THE DARKENED BEDROOM,
VI-A-GA-RA
TONIGHT!
IN THE BEDROOM
THE DARKENED BEDROOM
VI-A-GA-RA
TONIGHT!

MAN*:
VI-A-GA-RA, VI-A-GA-RA,
VI-A-GA-RA, VI-A-GA-RA,
VI-A-GA-RA, VI-A-GA-RA,
VI-A-GA-RA, VI-A-GA-RA,
VI-A-GA-RA, VI-A-GA-RA,
VI-A-GA-RA, VI-A-GA-RA,
VI-A-GA-RA, VI-A-GA-RA,
VI-A-GA-RA, VI-A-GA-RA,

VI-A-GA-RA, VI-A-GA-RA,
VI-A-GA-RA, VI-A-GA-RA,
VI-A-GA-RA, VI-A-GA-RA,
VI-A-GA-RA, VI-A-GA-RA,

MAN (CONT'D)*:
>VI-A-GA-RA, VI-A-GA-RA,
>VI-A-GA-RA, VI-A-GA-RA,
>VI-A-GA-RA, VI-A-GA-RA,
>VI-A-GA-RA,

WOMAN:
>UP, UP AND AWAY-AY-AY WITH HIS BEAUTIFUL,
>HIS BEAUTIFUL BLUE PILL.

>VIAGRA, WHOA, WHOA. VIAGRA,
>IT NEVER SAYS NO.

MAN:
>VIAGRA, VIAGRA. THAT LITTLE BLUE PILL, THAT LITTLE BLUE PILL
>VIAGRA, VIAGRA. IT'LL GIVE YA A THRILL.

>VIAGRA. I JUST TOOK A PILL CALLED VIAGRA.

WOMAN & MAN:
>I GET BY
>WITH A LITTLE HELP
>FROM MY PILL.
>OOH
>GONNA TRY
>WITH A LITTLE HELP
>FROM MY PILL.
>OOOO
>MAKE IT HIGH
>WITH A LITTLE HELP
>FROM MY PILL.

WOMAN (*opens pill bottle, takes out blue balloon and hands it to Man*):
>WHEN YOU GET OLD AND THINGS JUST FOLD,
>DON'T JUMP OFF NIAGRA.
>PRESCRIPTION FILLED,
>JUST TAKE THE PILL,
>THE PILL THEY CALL VIAGRA.

>>*MAN blows up balloon.*

>VIAGRA. VIAGRA.
>THEY CALL THE PILL VIAGRA.

>>*MAN releases blown up balloon.*

MAN:
>I FOUND MY THRILL, WITH A LITTLE BLUE PILL.

WOMAN:
VIAGRA'S BACK GONNA GET A LITTLE ACTION.

WOMAN & MAN:
HEY LA, HEY LA.

VIAGRA'S BACK.

WOMAN:
THE LAST TIME IT WAS HERE I ENDED UP IN TRACTION.

WOMAN & MAN:
HEY LA, HEY LA.

VIAGRA'S BACK.

THERE'S NO AGRA

LIKE VI-AGRA

LIKE NO AGRA I KNOW.

WOMAN:
IF YOU ARE DECEMBER AND YOUR MATE IS MAY,

MAN:
IT WORKS WHETHER YOU'RE STRAIGHT OR GAY.

WOMAN & MAN:
THANKS FOR THE APPROVAL

FROM THE F-D-A.

IT WORKS

WHEN SHE SAYS I WILL.

VIAGRA,

THE LITTLE BLUE PILL.

> *Both fire poppers. MAN's fails.*

> *Caesura.*

WOMAN: That's ok. It happens to everybody.

> *(Singing)*
UP UP AND AWAY

SCENE 26

MAN: Remember the day we first thought of moving to Pelican Roost?

    (Singing)
EVERYDAY IN OUR MAILBOX AT QUARTER PAST THREE.
E-Z CREDIT, PUBLISHERS CLEARINGHOUSE, SAVE THE CHIMPANZEES.
ONE DAY AMONGST THE JUNK MAIL, COULD IT BE FOR ME?
AN INVITATION TO BELONG TO THE AARP.

    Simultaneously.

MAN:
IT IS FOR ME!
FINALLY!
HONESTLY
YA WANNA SEE?
FOR ONE LOW FEE!
FRE-E-E.

WOMAN:
AARP
AARP
AARP
AARP
AARP
YOUR SPOUSE IS FREE-E-E...

MAN & WOMAN:
YOU GET EVERYTHING YA NEED FROM THE AARP.

MAN:
I OPENED UP THE MAILER AND INSIDE WAS THIS PLEA:
DID I WANT TO LIVE IN COMFORT AND AGE WITH DIGNITY?
DON'T BE A BURDEN TO OUR KIDS AND TO SOCIETY?
I SIGNED UP THEN AND THERE, AND NOW THEY'RE SENDIN' ME!

    Simultaneously.

MAN*:
A RECIPE.
SOME HERBAL TEAS
A CURE FOR FLEAS.
NEW BVDS
A PHD!?!
FREE-E-E

WOMAN*:
>AARP
>
>AARP
>
>AARP
>
>AARP
>
>AARP
>
>AND IT'S ALL FREE-E-E...

MAN & WOMAN:
>YOU GET EVERYTHING YA NEED FROM THE AARP

MAN (rubato— slow— with feeling):
>SO IF YOU'RE WONDERING WHAT TO DO WHEN YOU START GETTIN' OLD.
>
>THERE'S A GROUP THAT'S GONNA HELP YA IF YOU STEP INTO THEIR FOLD.
>
>EV'RYDAY IN YOUR MAILBOX, YOUR COMPUTER AND TV.
>
>YOU'LL GET STACKS AND STACKS AND STACKS OF CRAP FROM THE AARP.

MAN & WOMAN:
>AARP
>
>EVERYBODY! / SING IT WITH ME!
>
>AARP
>
>AARP
>
>AARP
>
>ETERNALLY
>
>YOU'LL GET EVERYTHING YA WANT
>
>YOU'LL GET EVERYTHING YA LIKE
>
>YOU'LL GET EVERYTHING YA NEED
>
>FROM THE AARP.

>>*False church ending.*

>>*All music stops.*

>*(To audience)*

Thank you! Thank you!

>>*MAN and WOMAN turn and start to exit.*

MAN: One! Two! Three!

>>*MAN and WOMAN run back to places and sing, still call-response style, encouraging audience to sing along.*

MAN & WOMAN:
>AARP
>
>AARP
>
>AARP

MAN & WOMAN (CONT'D):
    AARP
    AARP
    FOR YOU AND ME-E-E
    YOU'LL GET EVERYTHING YA NEED FROM THE AARP.

SCENE 27

Ethereal music begins. Blue light floods the stage, we're back in... heaven.

MAN and WOMAN put on halos.

MAN: Pelican Roost really was the best years of our lives.

WOMAN:
I LOVED EVERY MINUTE.

MAN:
I HAD A GOOD TIME TOO.

WOMAN:
THE PEOPLE WHO WE MET.

MAN:
THE THINGS THEY WOULD DO.

WOMAN:
PELICAN ROOST WAS GREAT, IT WAS FUN TO LOOK BEHIND.

MAN & WOMAN:
IT'S MORE THAN JUST A PLACE, IT'S A STATE OF MIND.

Light change.

EVERYTHING IS SWELL WHEN YOU'RE IN PELICAN ROOST.
NO MATTER HOW YOU'RE DOIN' THEY'LL GIVE YA A BOOST.
LAUGHIN' AND LOVIN', ALWAYS SOMETHIN' TO DO.
WE HAVE EVERYTHING YOU WANT HERE AND IT'S WAITING FOR YOU.

EVERYTHING IS SWELL WHEN YOU'RE IN PELICAN ROOST.
EVERYONE WHO LIVES THERE IS THE TOPS.
WHEN WE HEAR THAT BELL A'TOLLIN'
WE'LL GO OUT ROCK-N-ROLLIN'.
EVR'YTHING IS PELICAN ROOST!

(Speaking)

See ya at The Roost!

ENCORE.

SONG #21: CHAPEL ABOVE

MAN & WOMAN:
> GOIN' TO THE CHAPEL AND I'M GONNA GET BURIED.
> GOIN' TO THE CHAPEL AND I'M GONNA GET BURIED.
> GEE, I'LL REALLY MISS YOU AND I'M GONNA GET BURIED.
> GOIN' TO THE CHAPEL ABOVE.
>
> I WENT TO SLEEP, LIKE I ALWAYS DO.
> I DIDN'T WAKE UP, THROUGH THE CEILING I FLEW.
> NOW I LOOK DOWN ON ALL OF YOU.
> PLEASE CANCEL MY COLONOSCOPY.
>
> GOIN' TO THE CHAPEL AND I'M GONNA GET BURIED.
> GOIN' TO THE CHAPEL AND I'M GONNA GET BURIED.
> GEE, I'LL REALLY MISS YOU AND I'M GONNA GET BURIED.
> GOIN' TO THE CHAPEL ABOVE.

WOMAN: Everybody sing! You know you wanna!

MAN & WOMAN (*clapping*):
> GOIN' TO THE CHAPEL AND I'M GONNA GET BURIED.
> GOIN' TO THE CHAPEL AND I'M GONNA GET BURIED.
> GEE, I'LL REALLY MISS YOU AND I'M GONNA GET BURIED.
> GOIN' TO THE CHAPEL ABOVE.

WOMAN: I'll keep a light on.

MAN & WOMAN:
> GOIN' TO THE CHAPEL ABOVE.

MAN: Don't skip confession.

MAN & WOMAN:
> GOIN' TO THE CHAPEL ABOVE.

THE END

ABOUT STAGE RIGHTS

Based in Los Angeles and founded in 2000, Stage Rights is one of the foremost independent theatrical publishers in the United States, providing stage performance rights for a wide range of plays and musicals to theater companies, schools, and other producing organizations across the country and internationally. As a licensing agent, Stage Rights is committed to providing each producer the tools they need for financial and artistic success. Stage Rights is dedicated to the future of live theatre, offering special programs that champion new theatrical works.

To view all of our current plays and musicals, visit:

www.stagerights.com

Made in the USA
San Bernardino, CA
22 February 2020